MW01537284

This Coloring Book Belongs To:

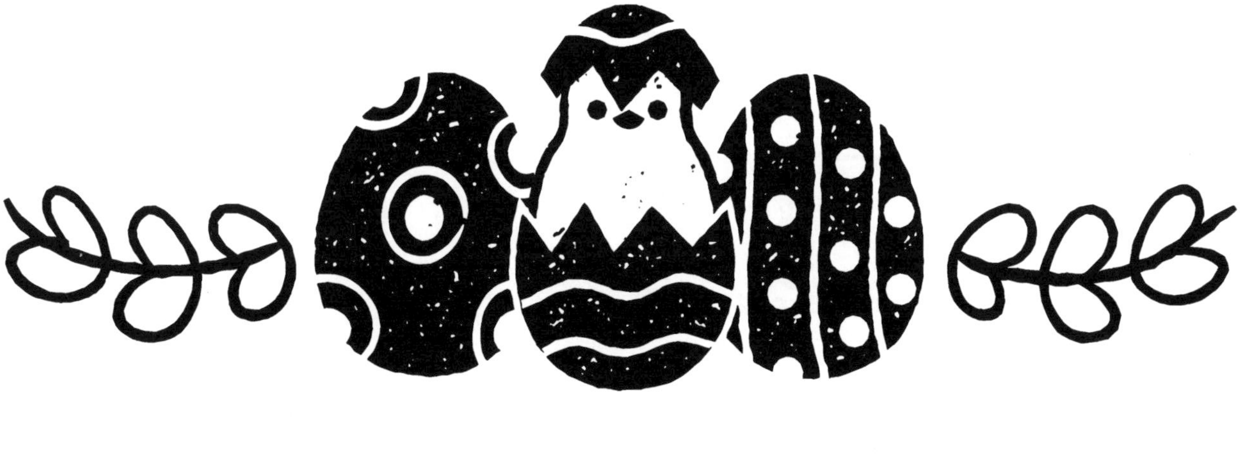

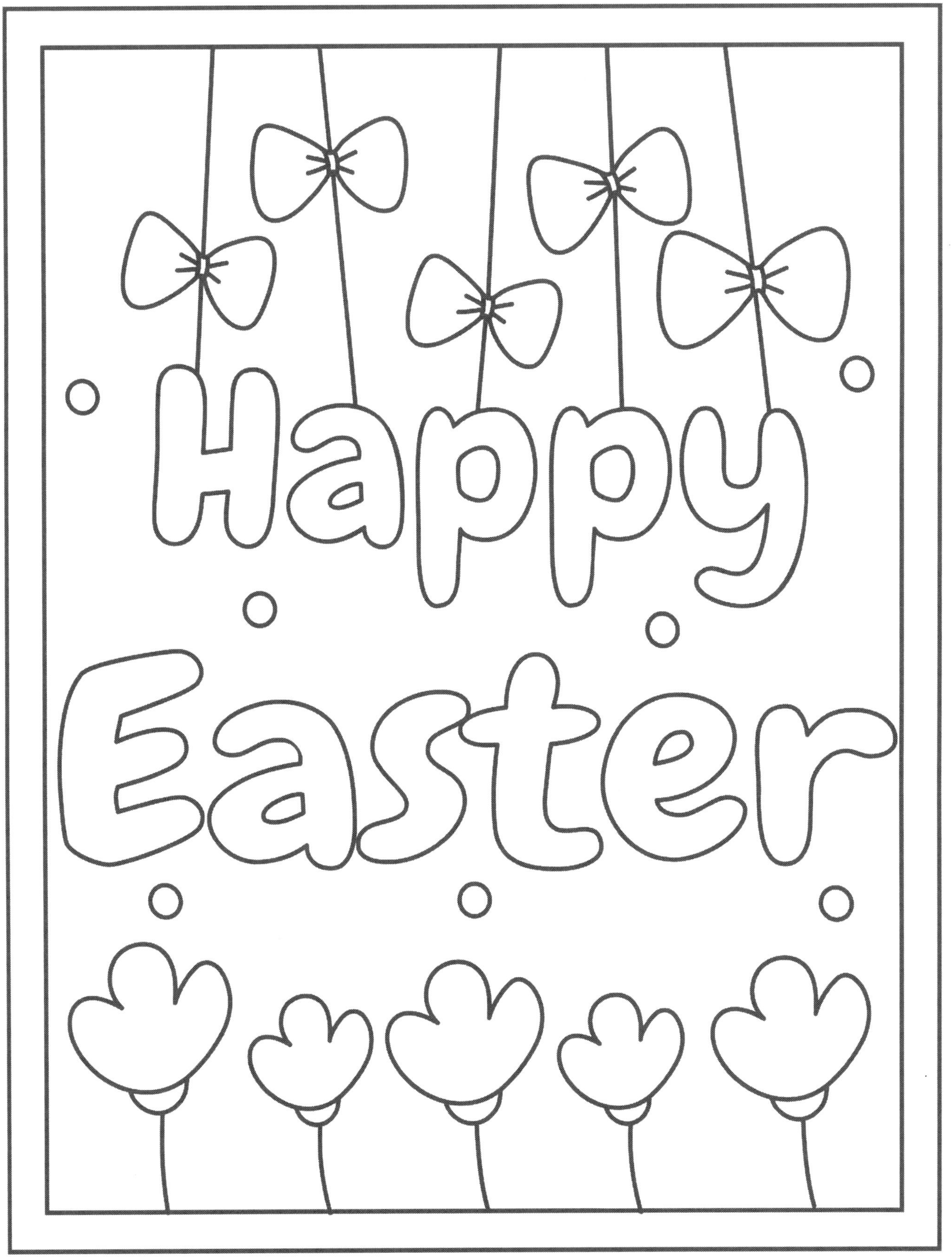
Happy
Easter

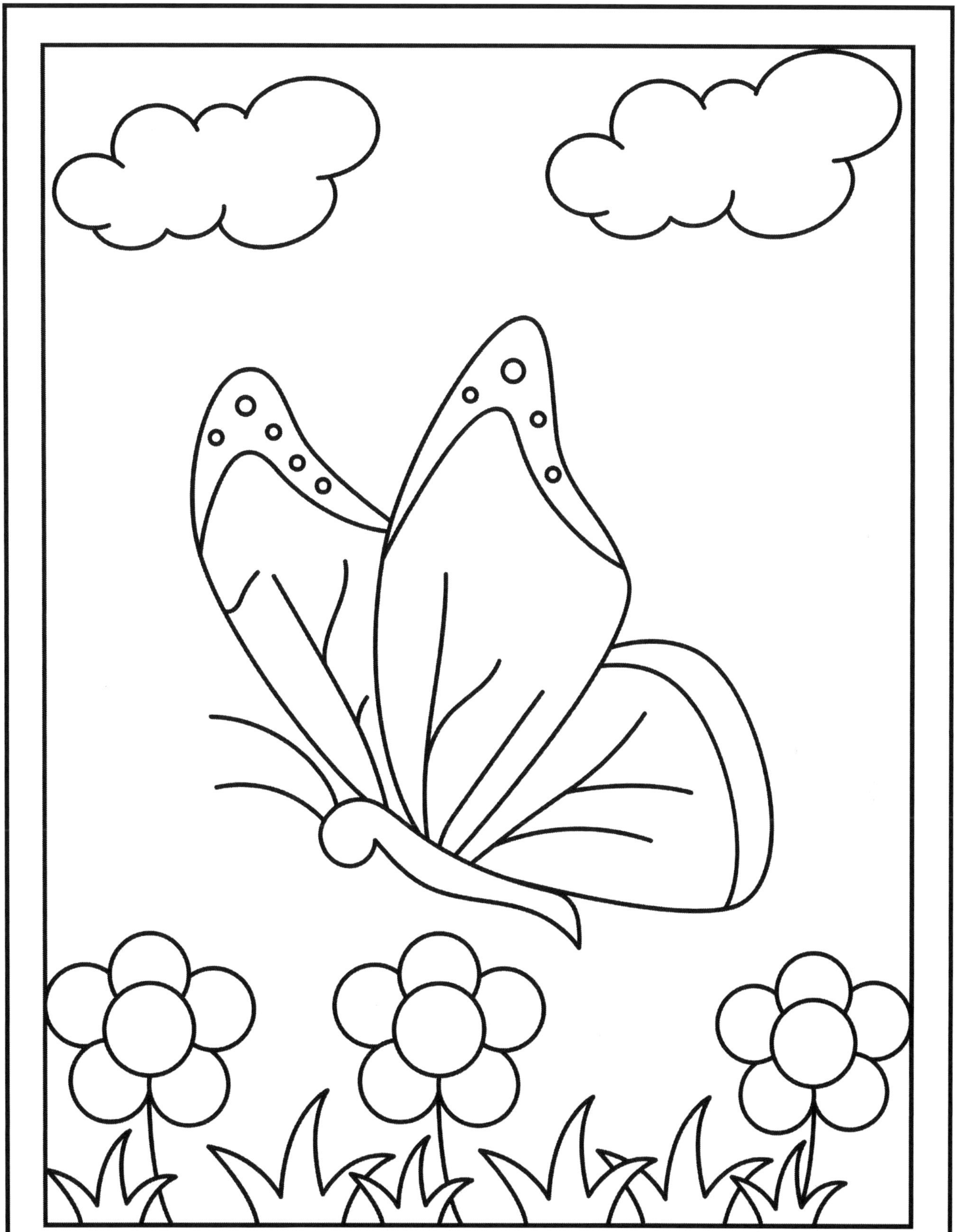

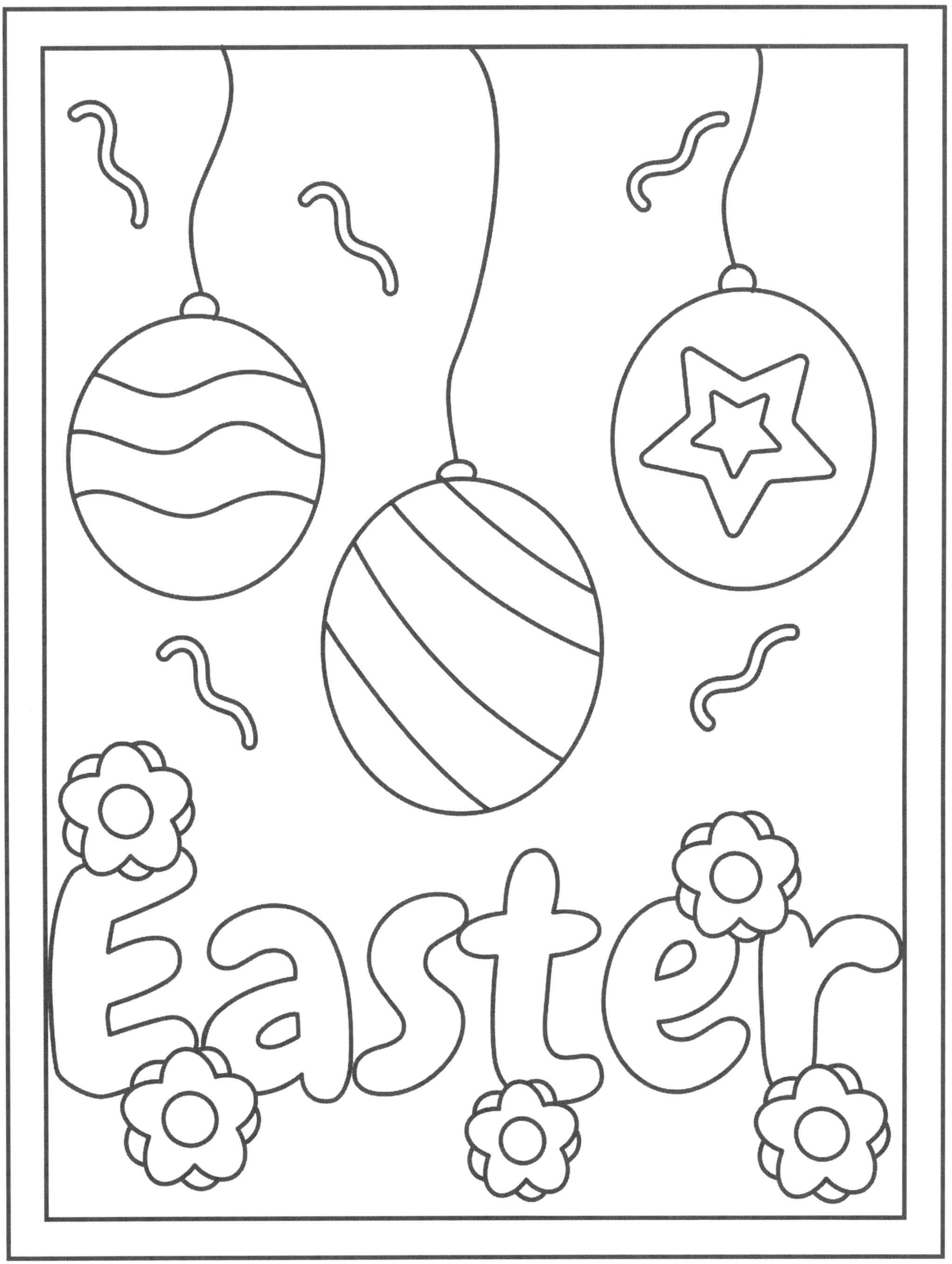
Easter

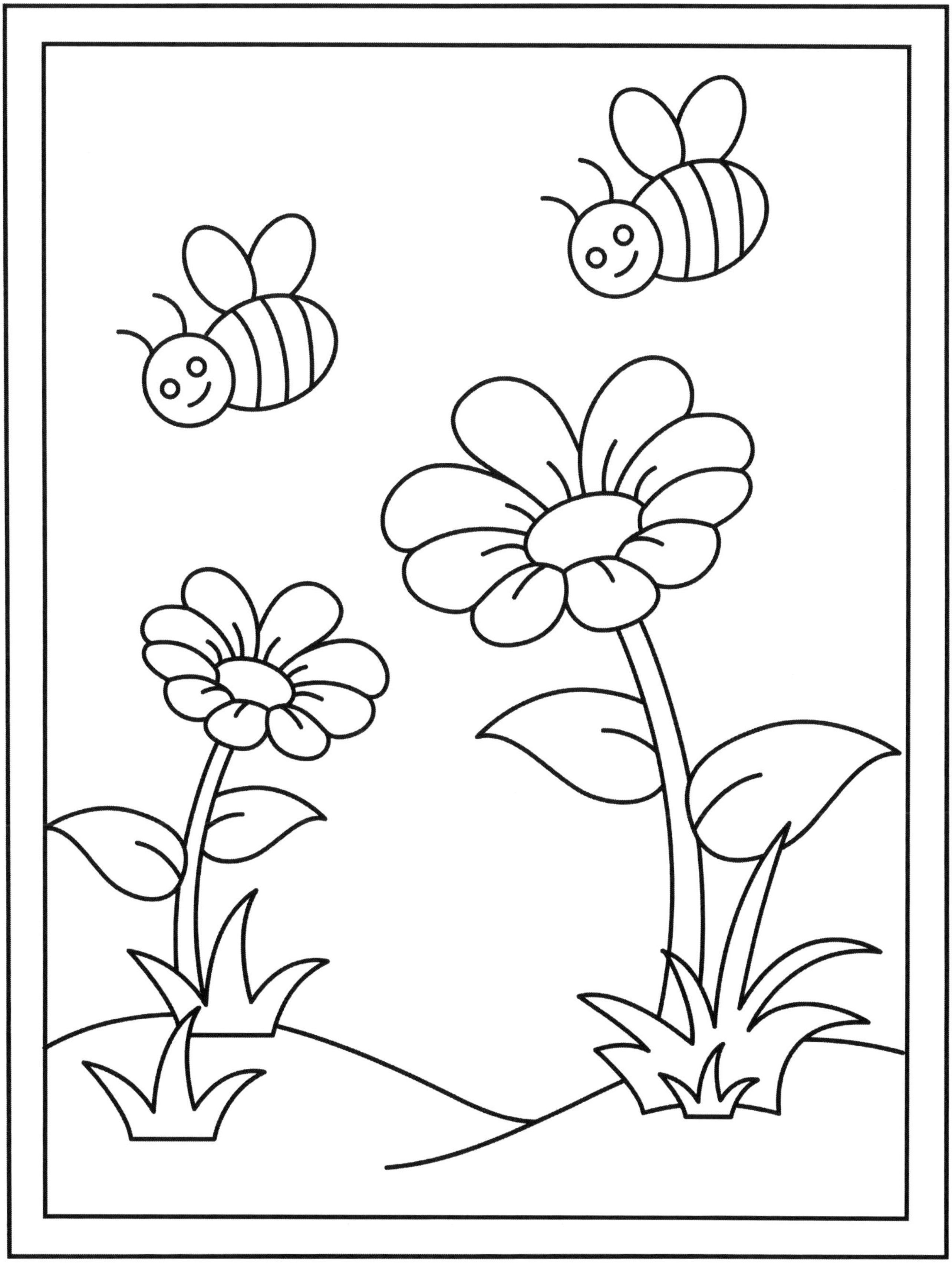

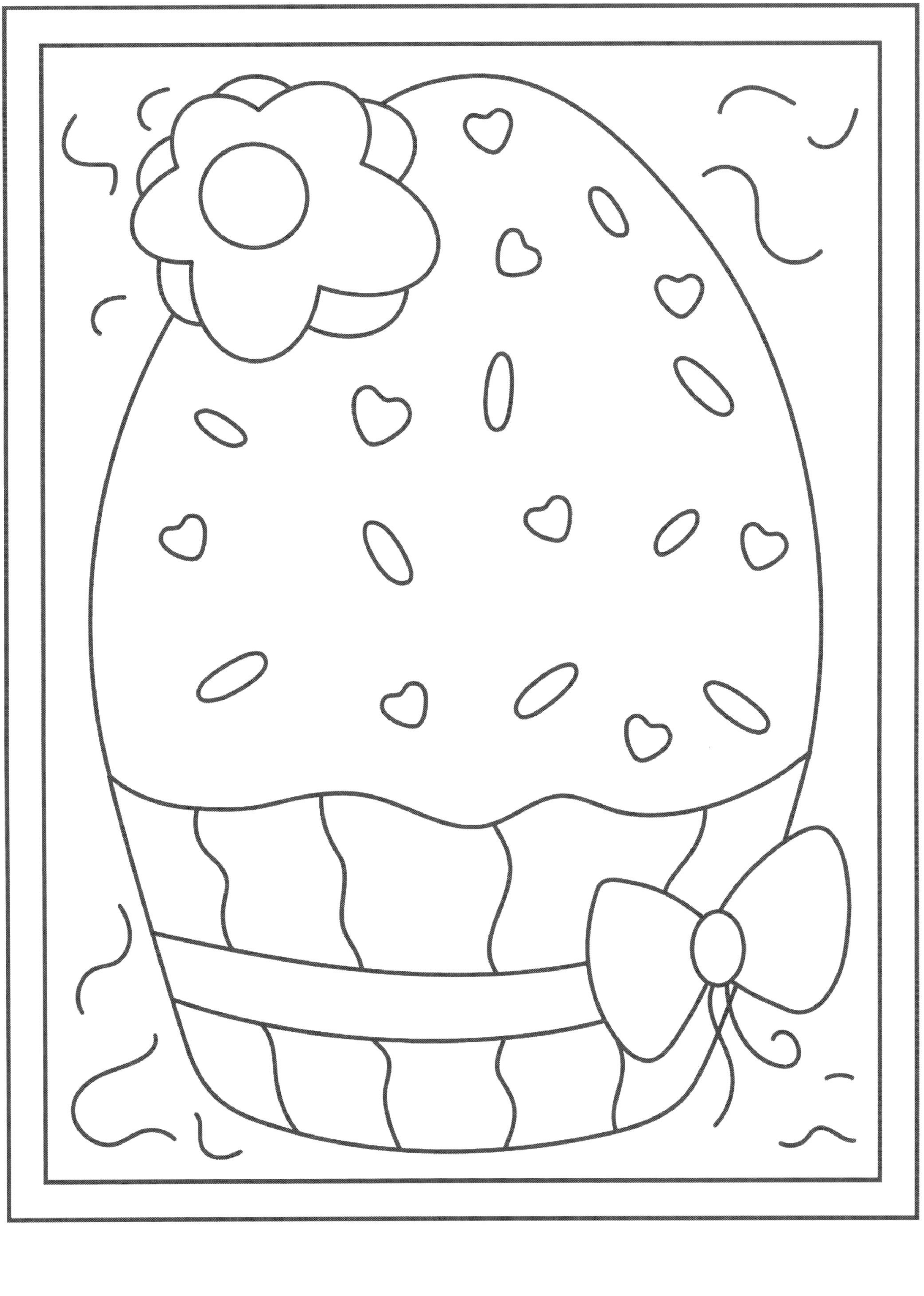

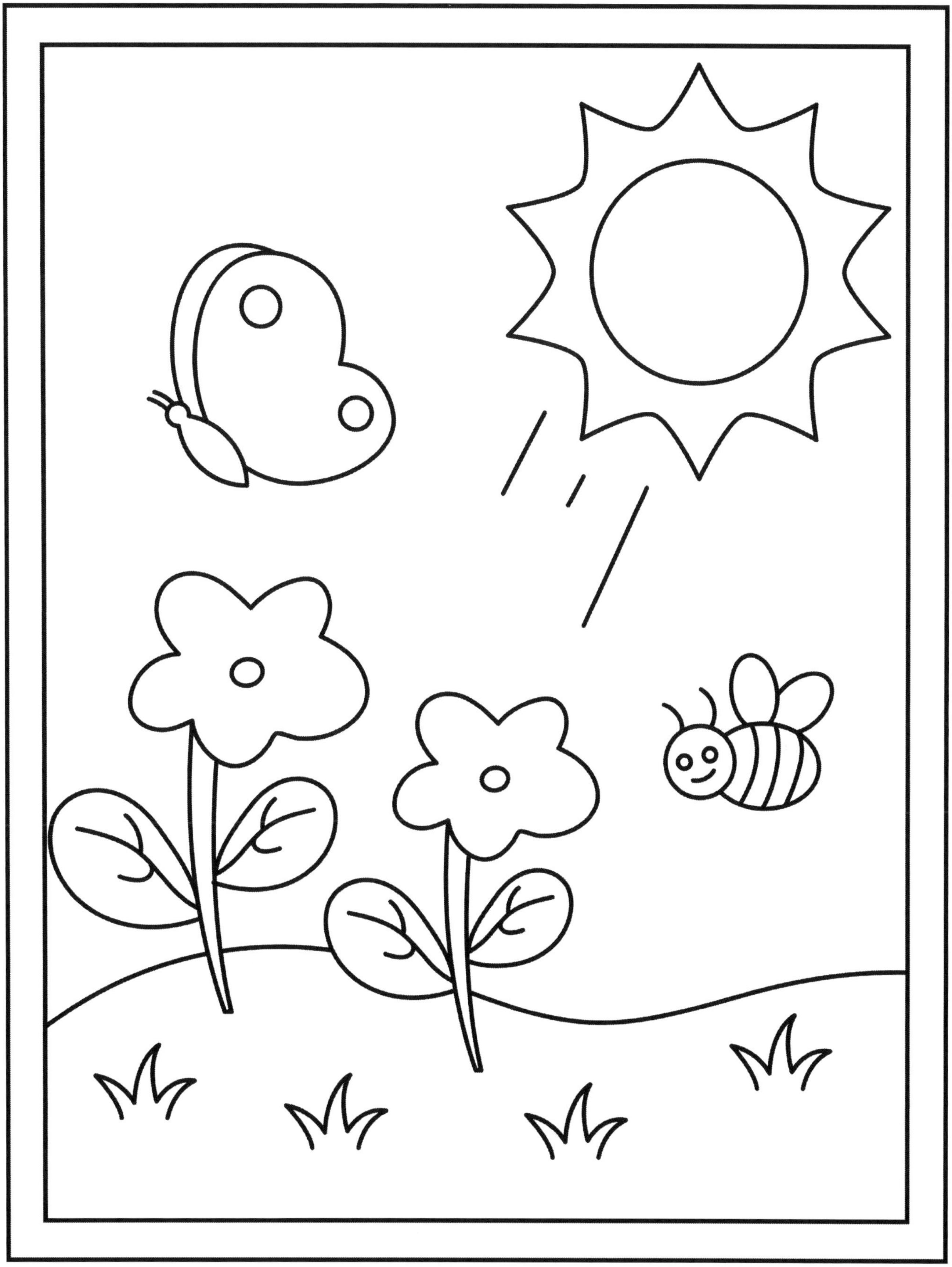

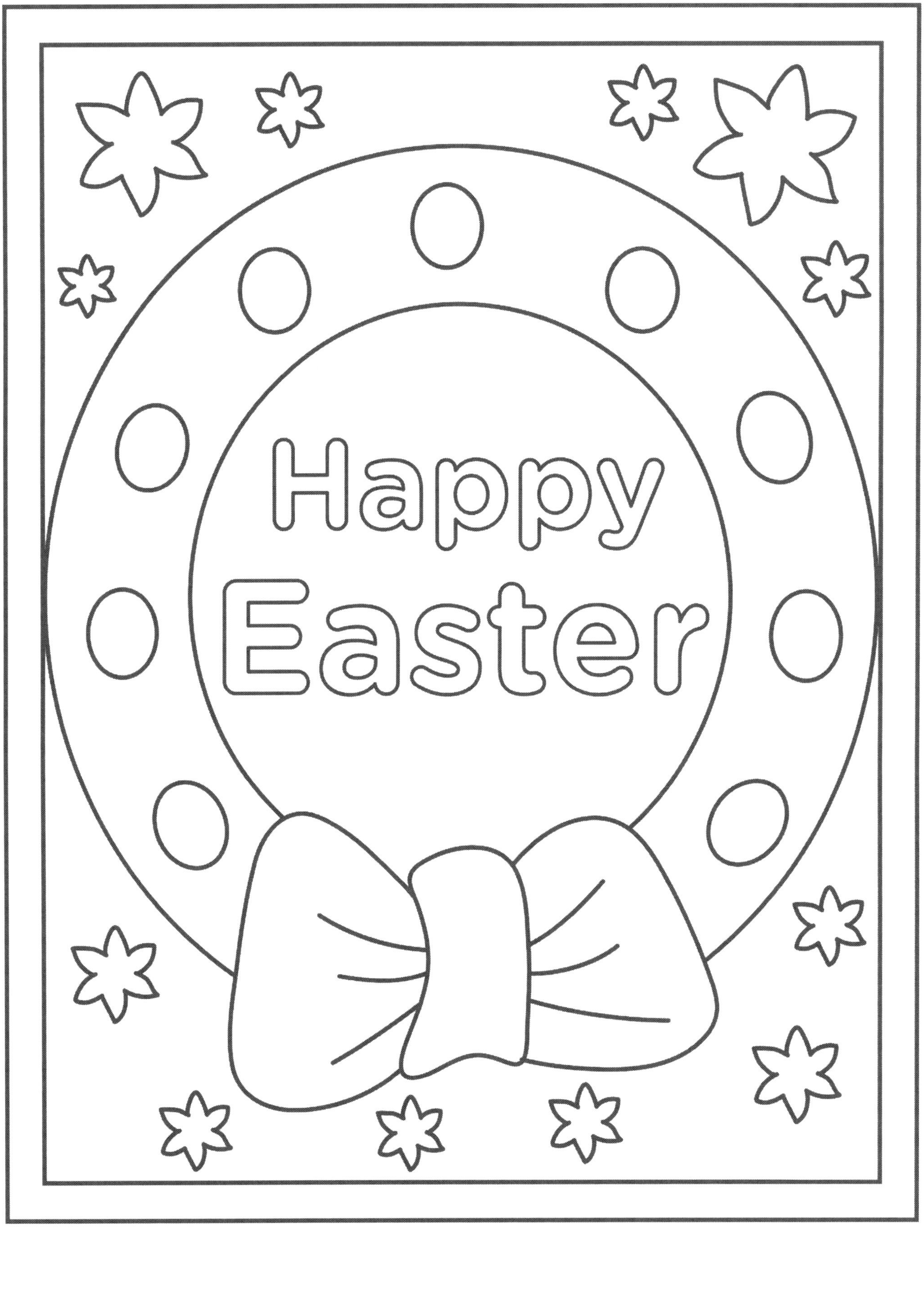
Happy
Easter

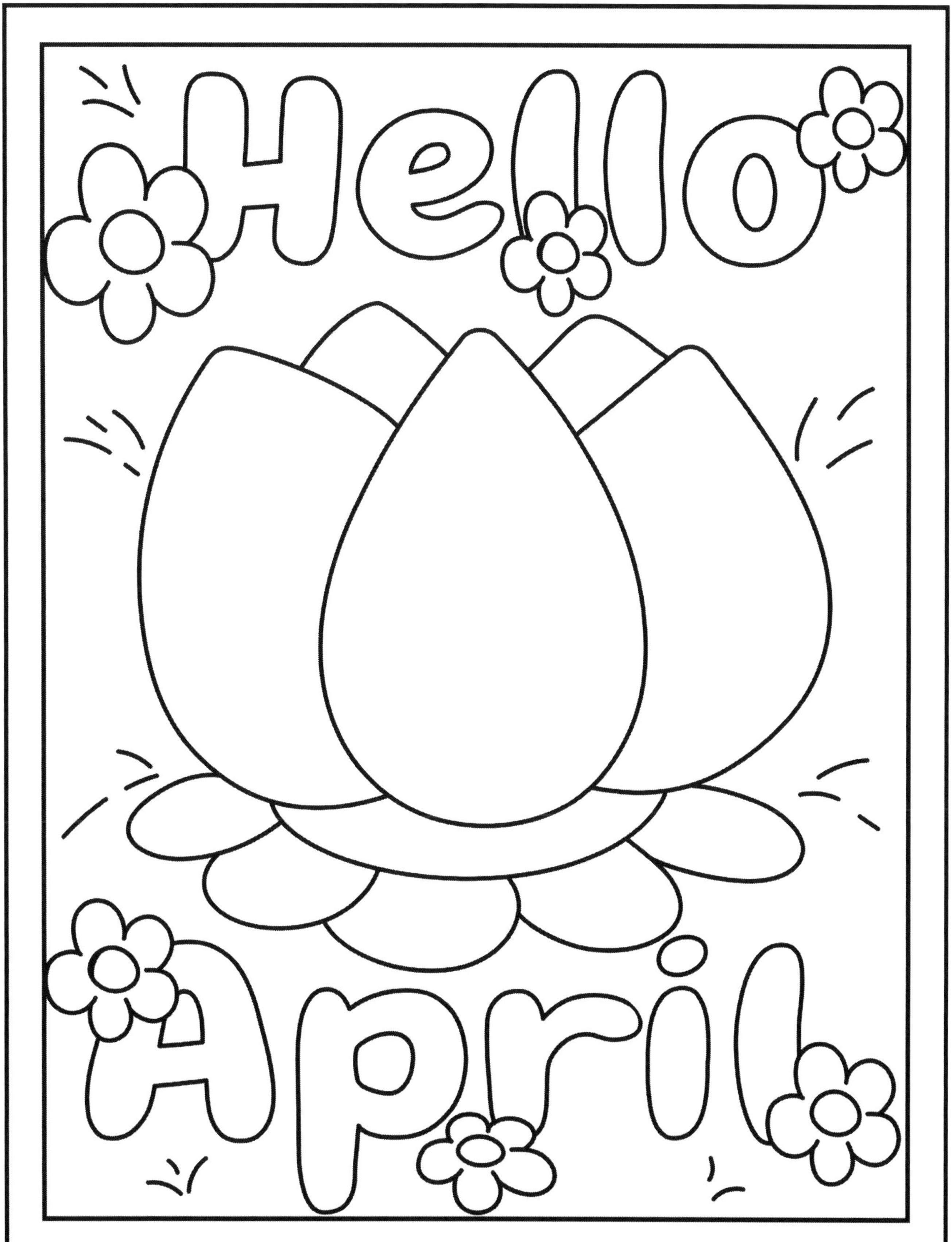
Hello
April

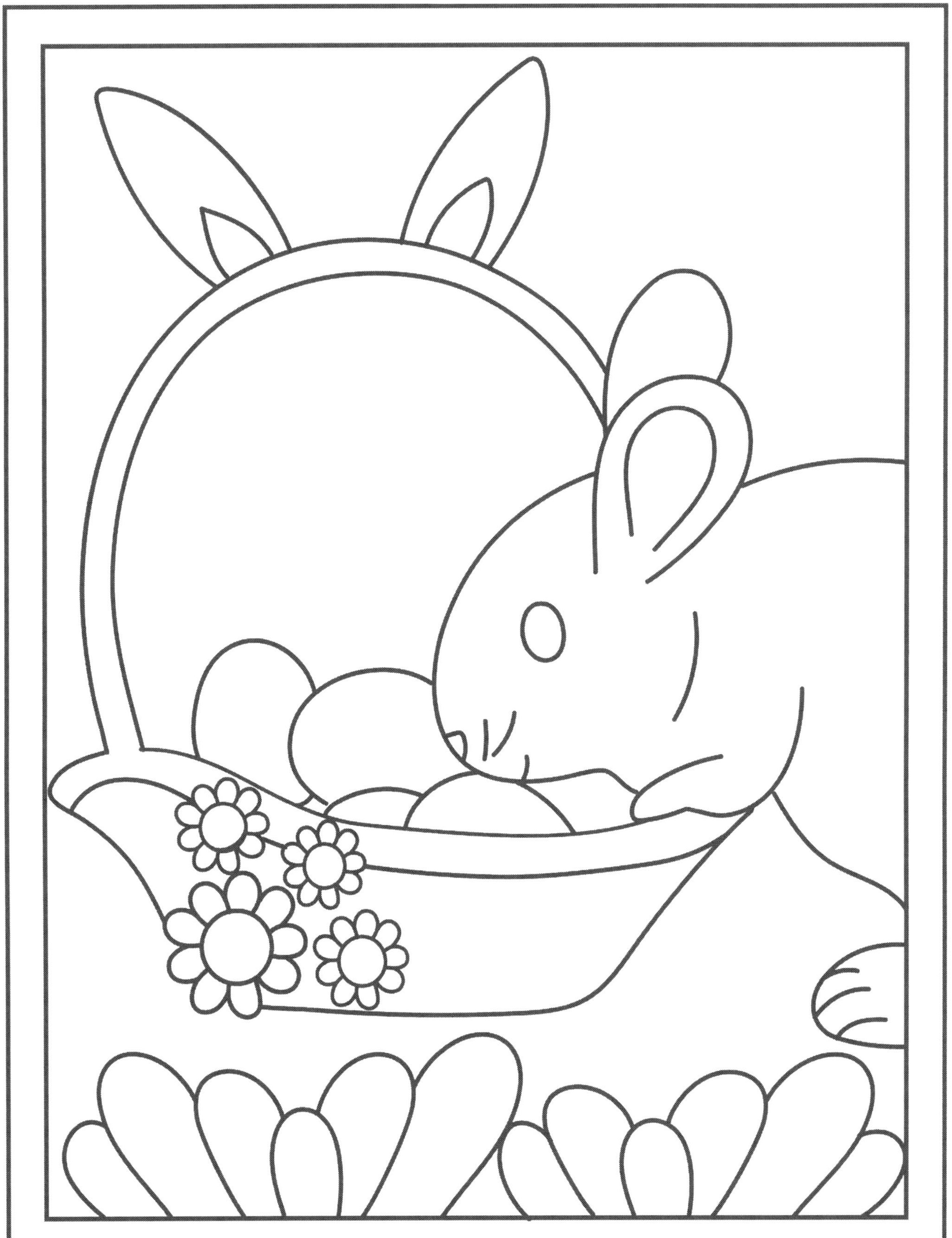

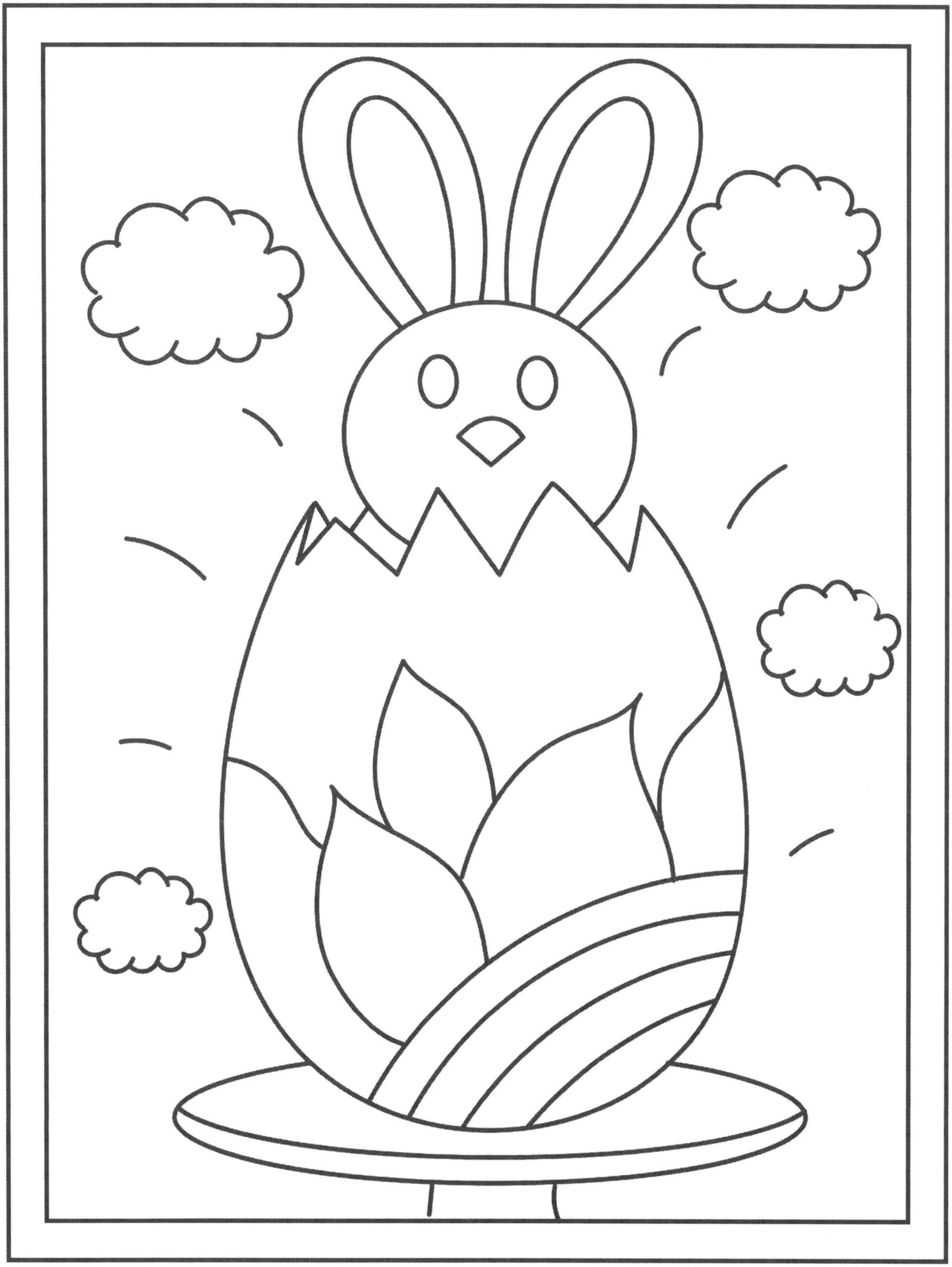

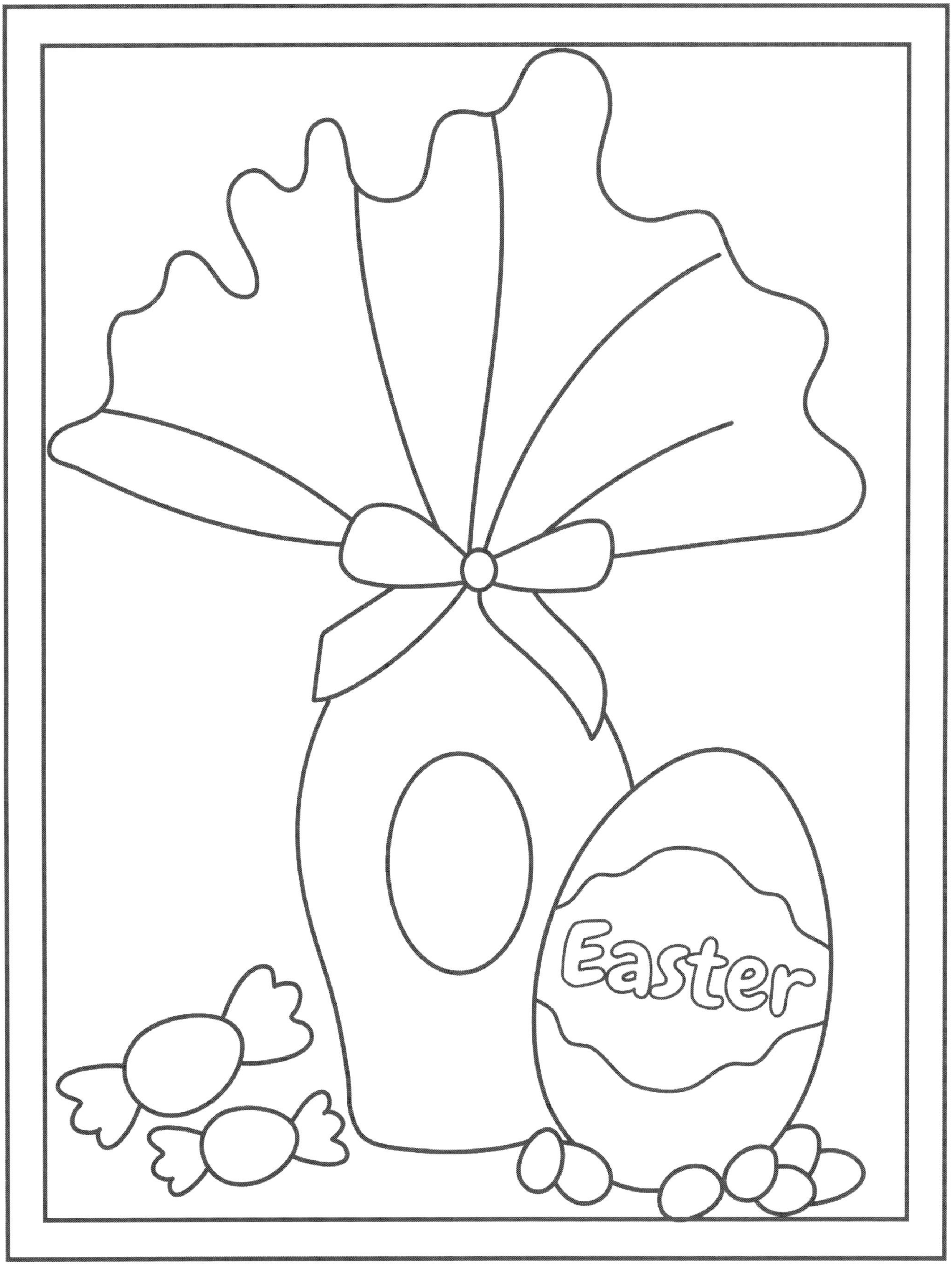
Easter

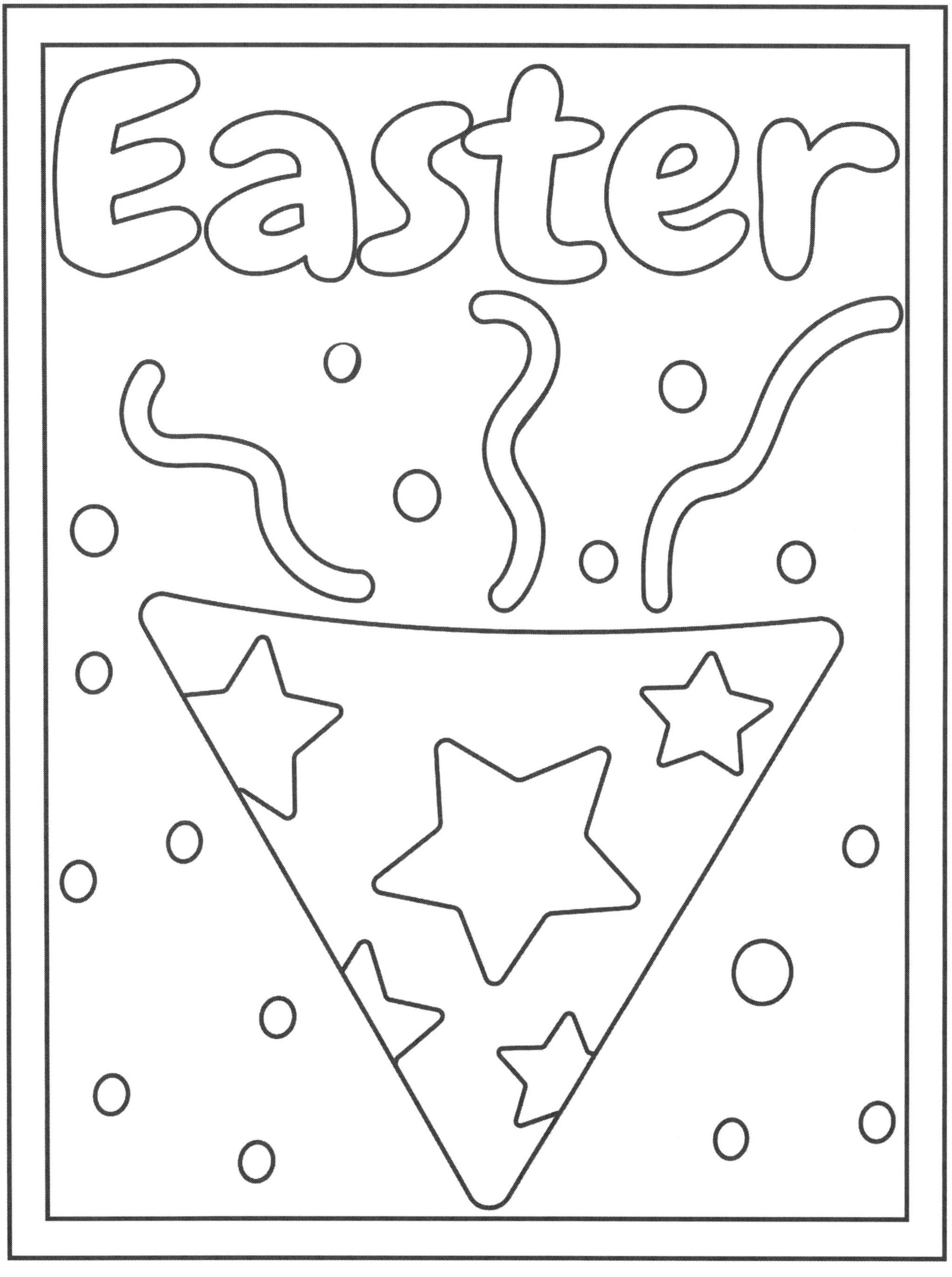
Easter

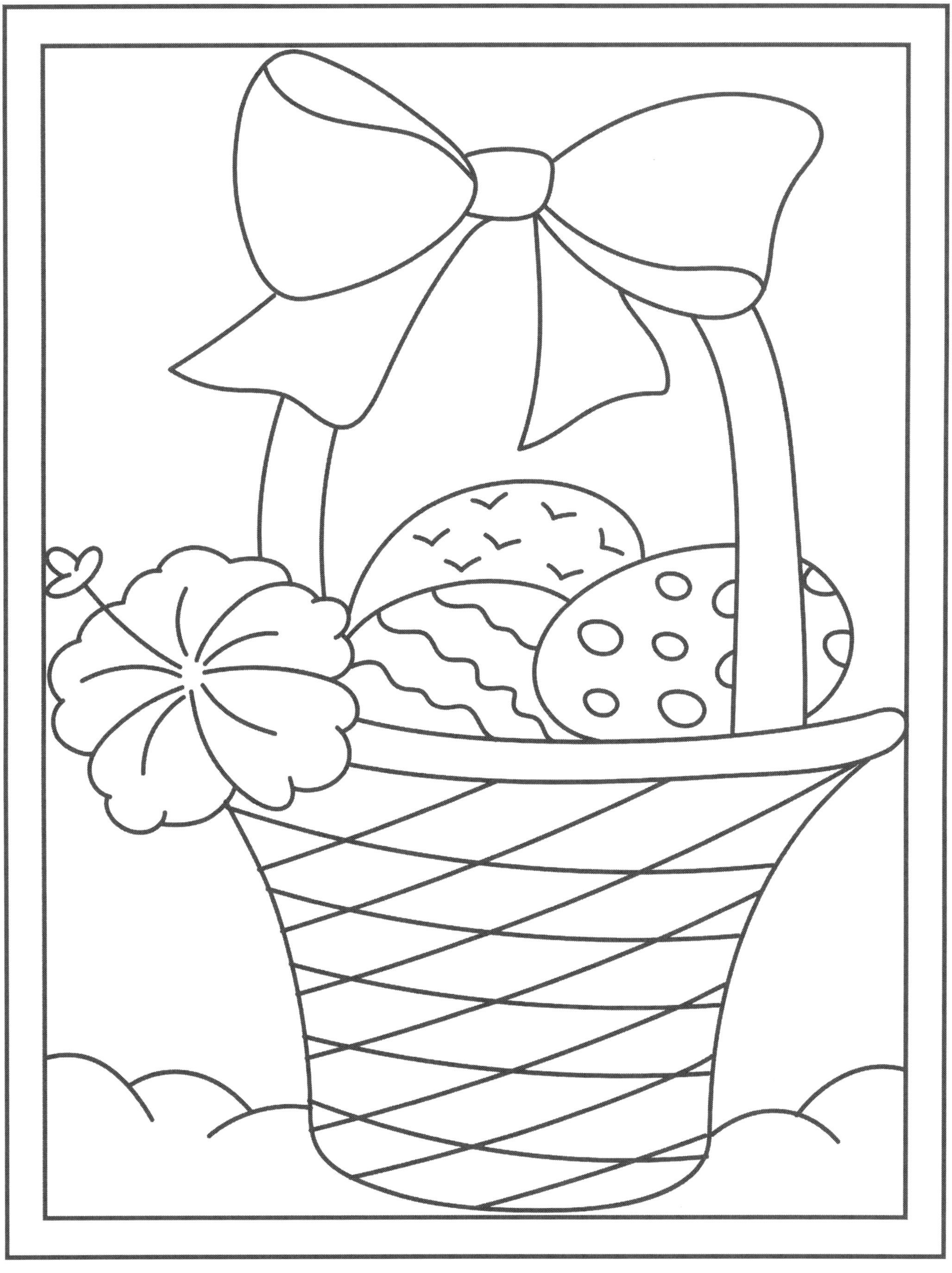

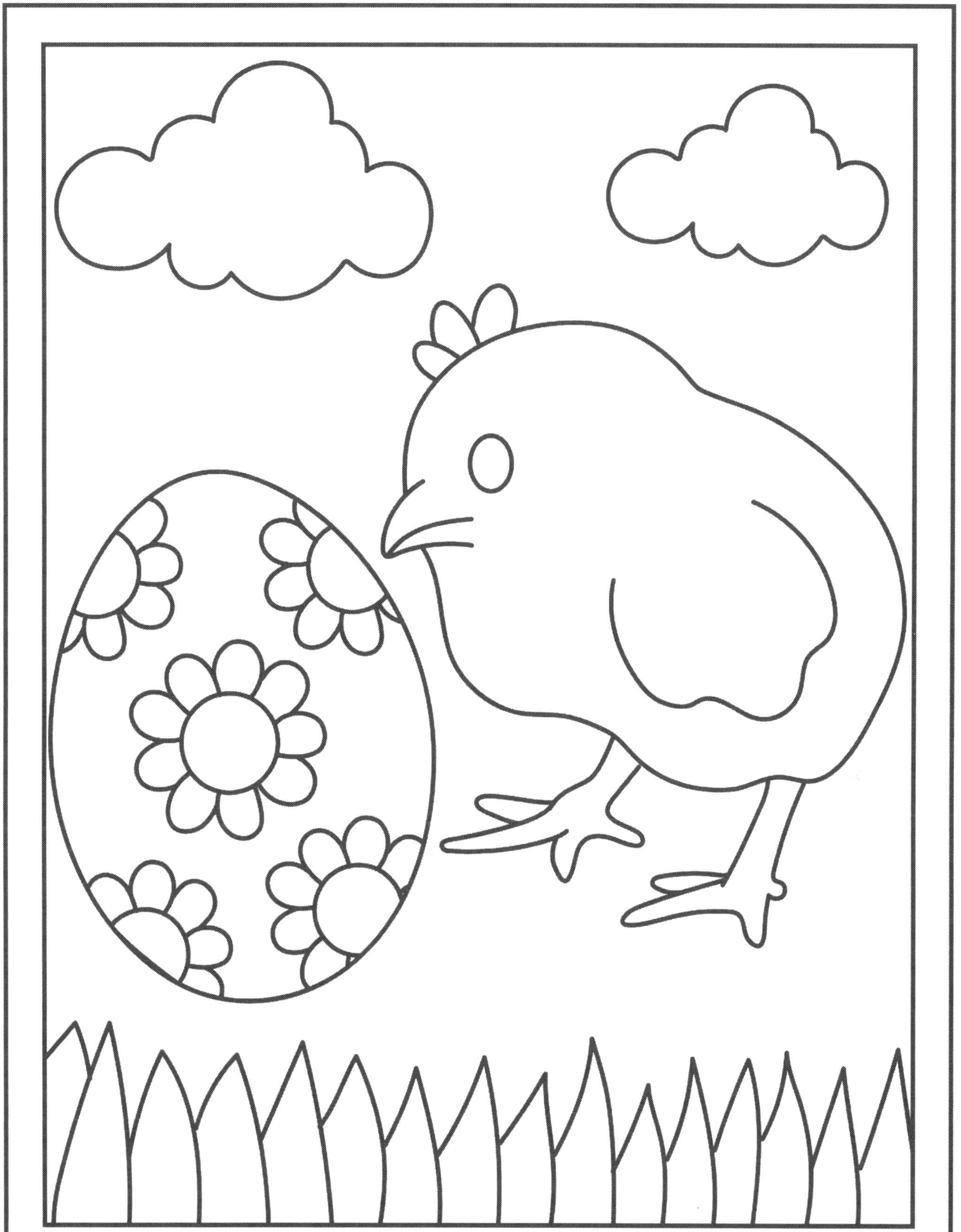

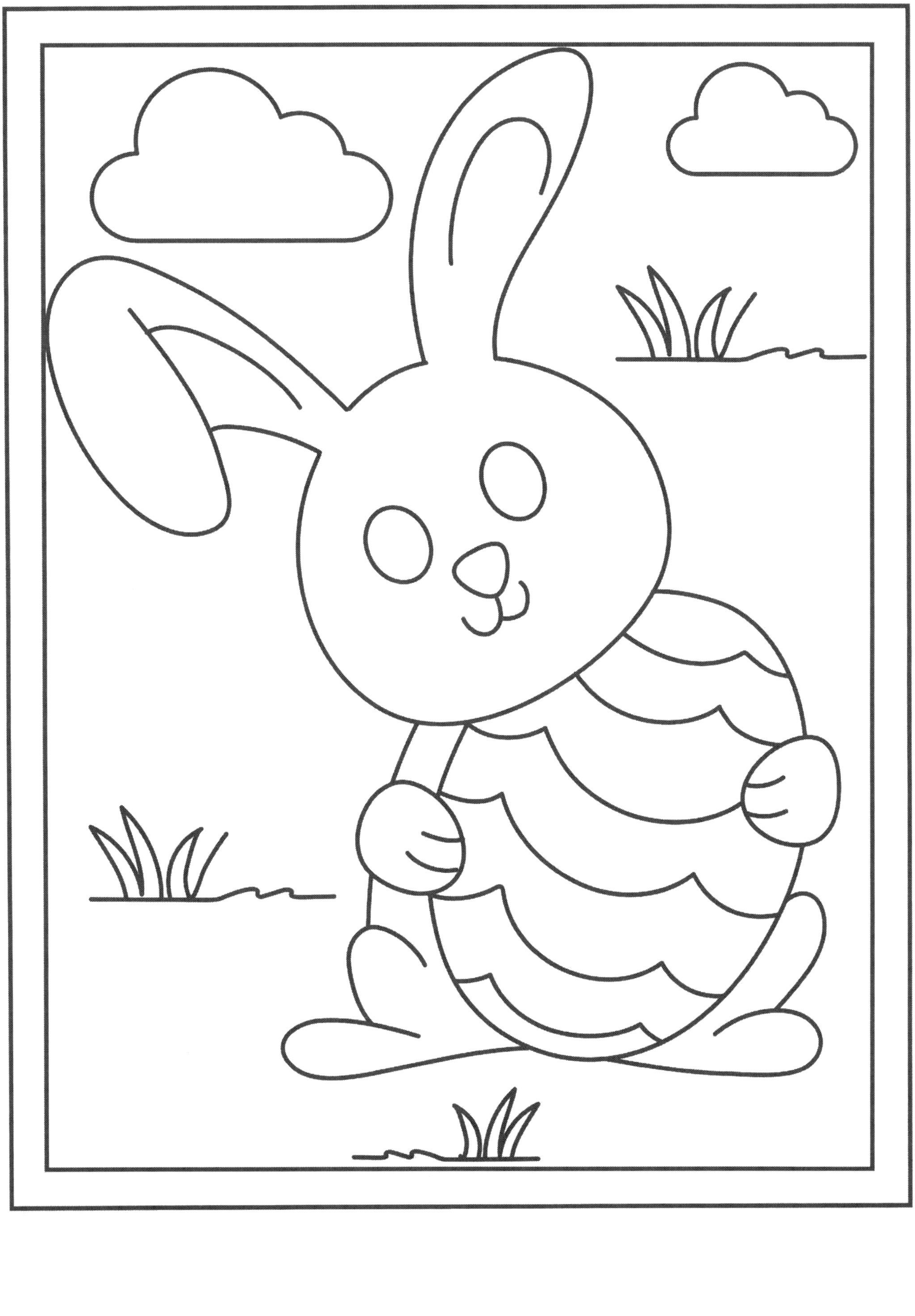

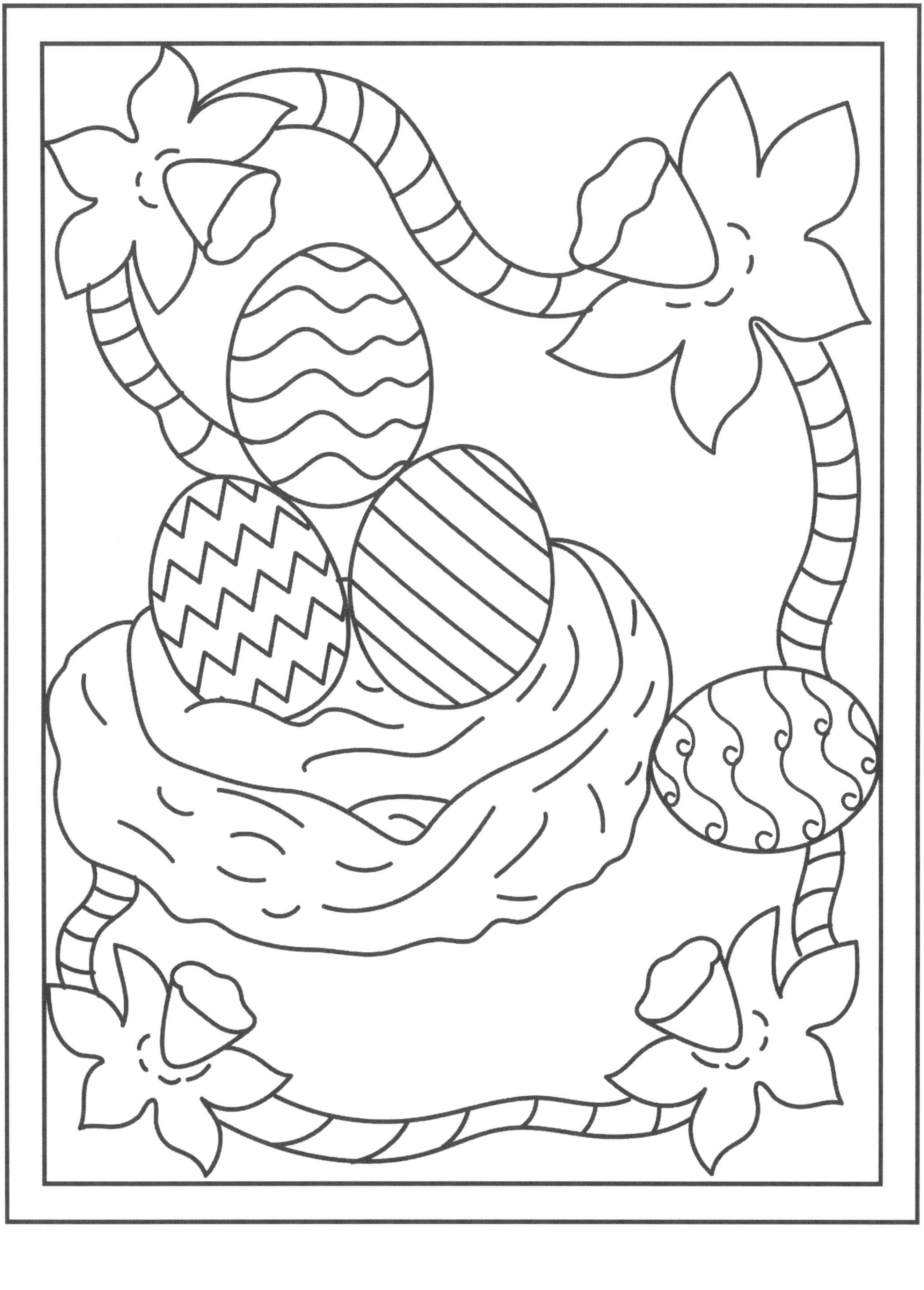

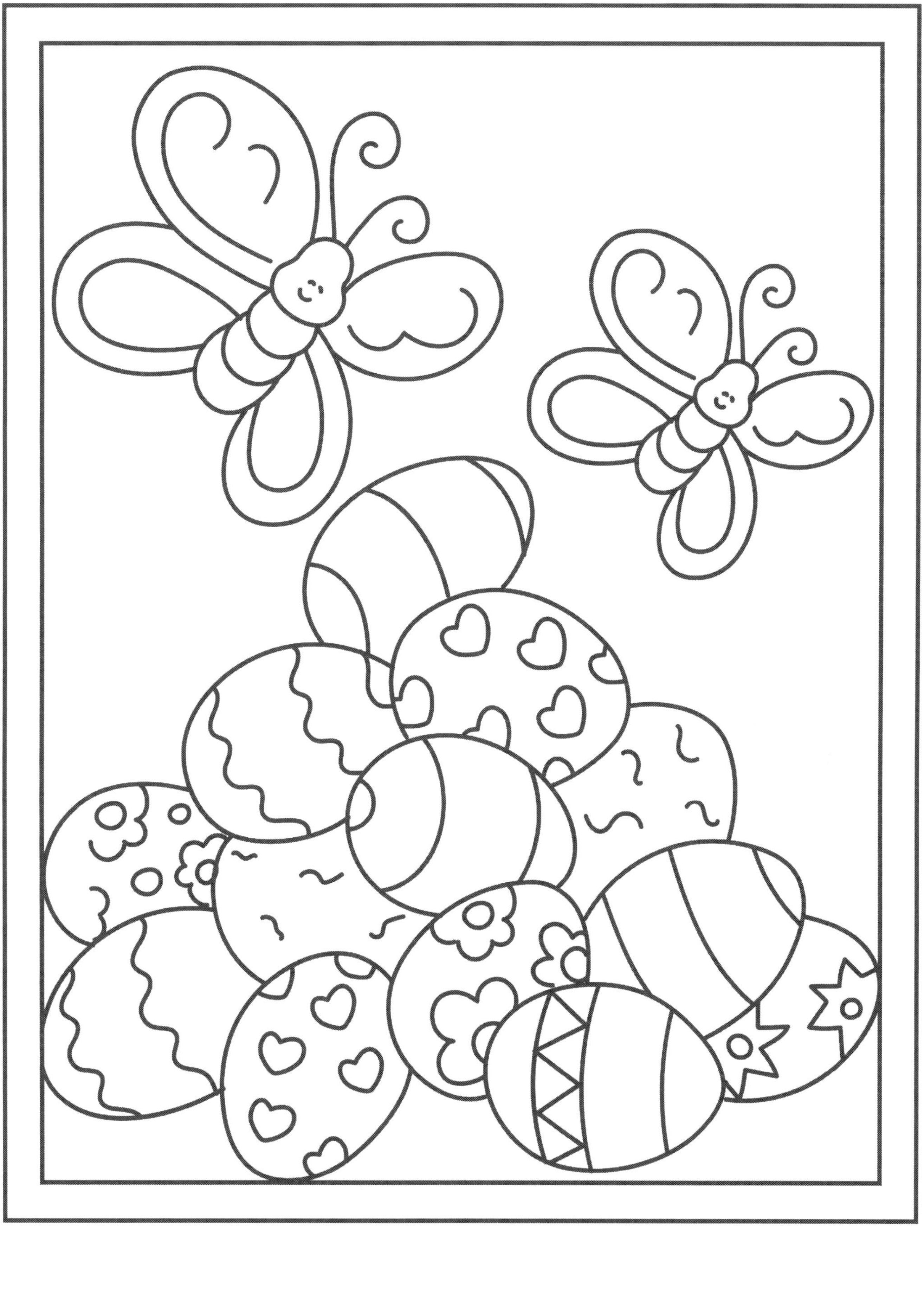

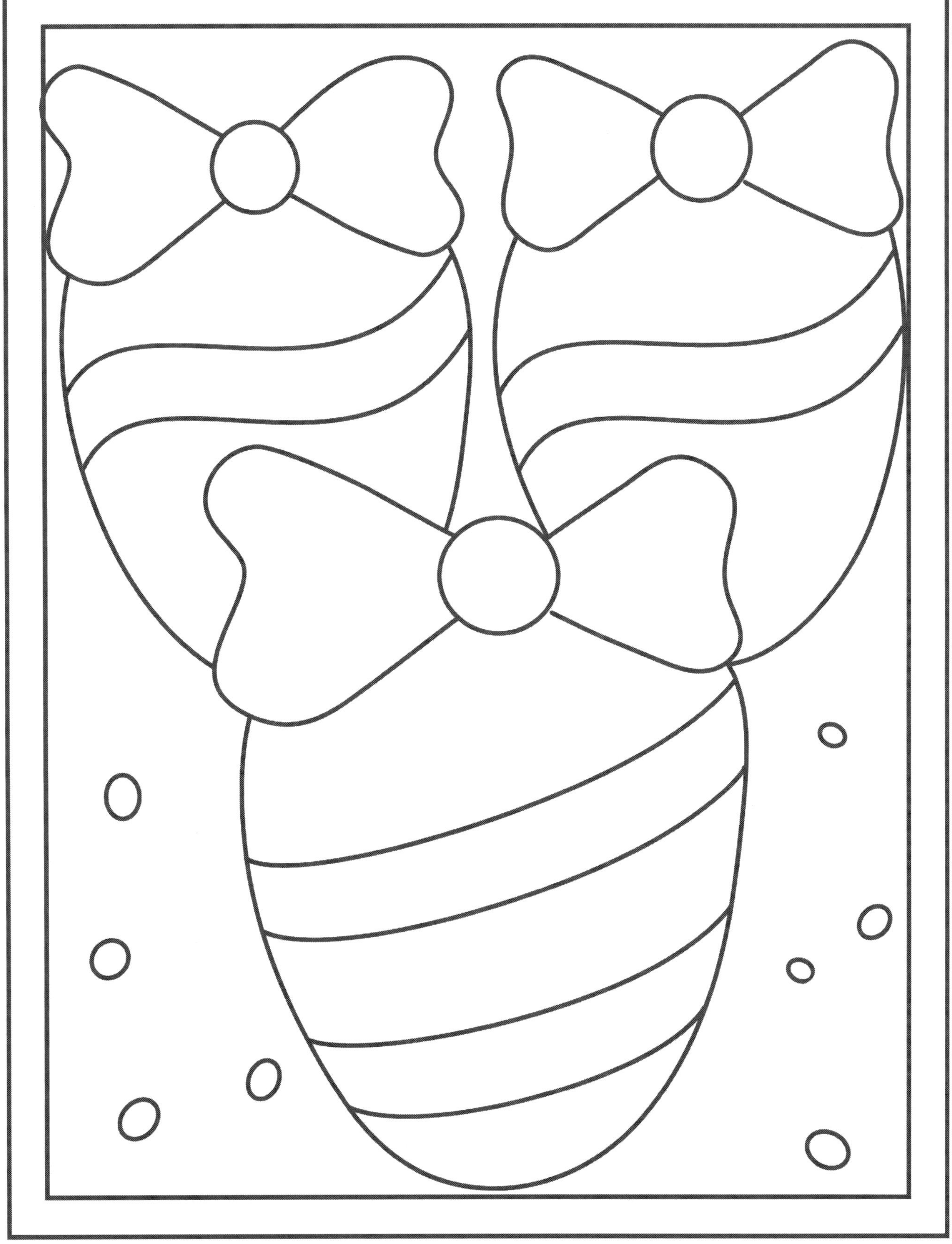

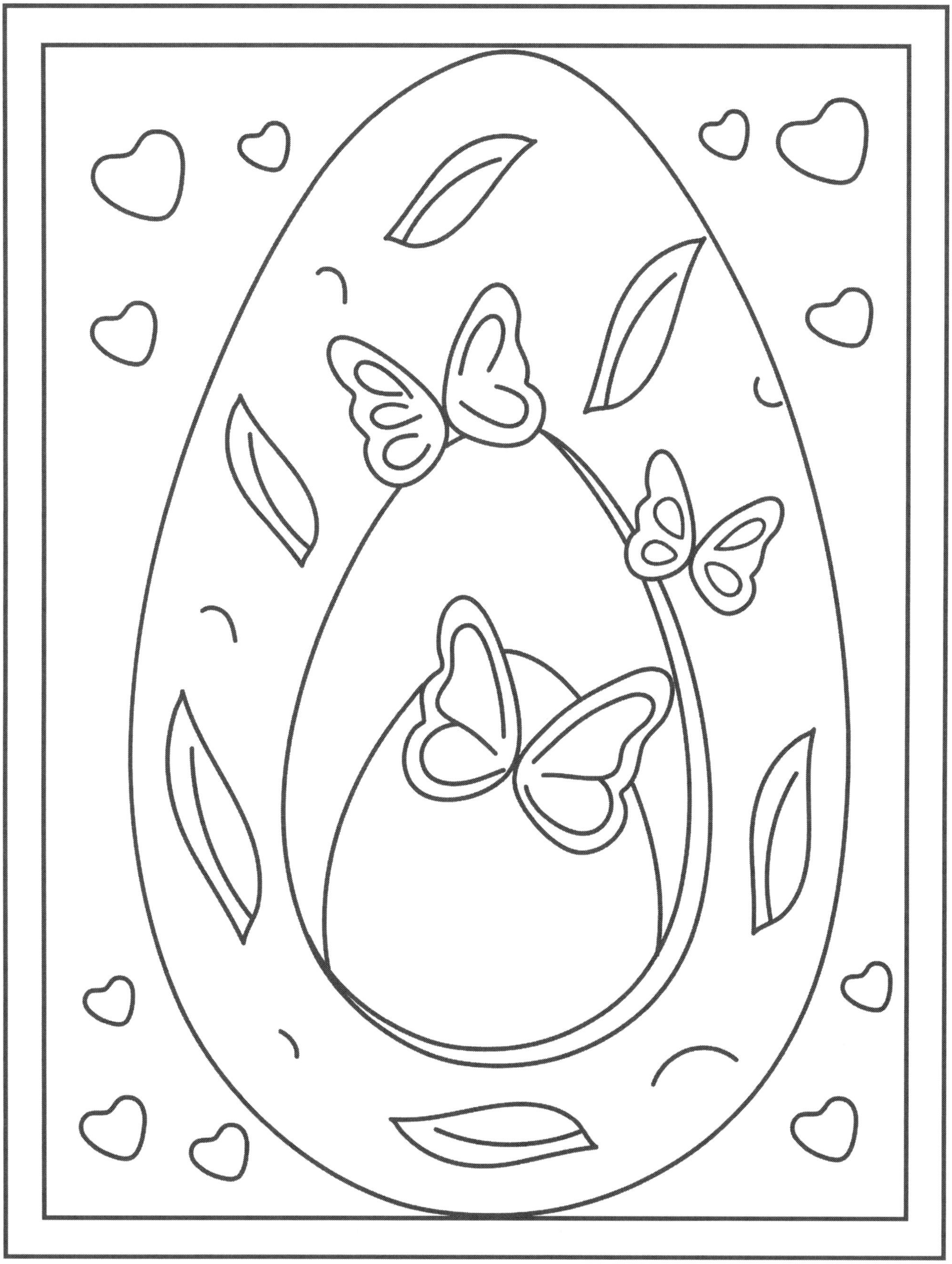

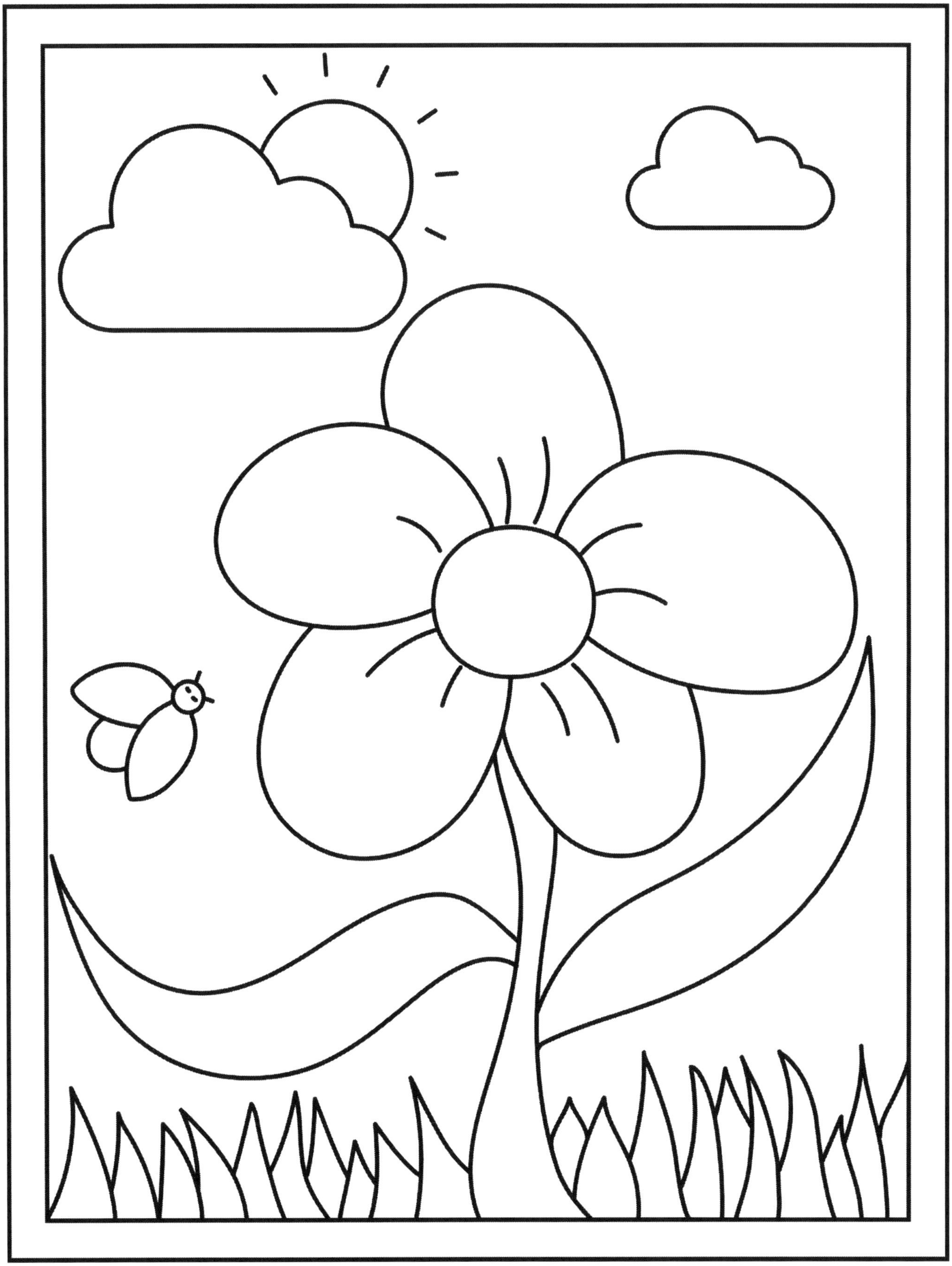

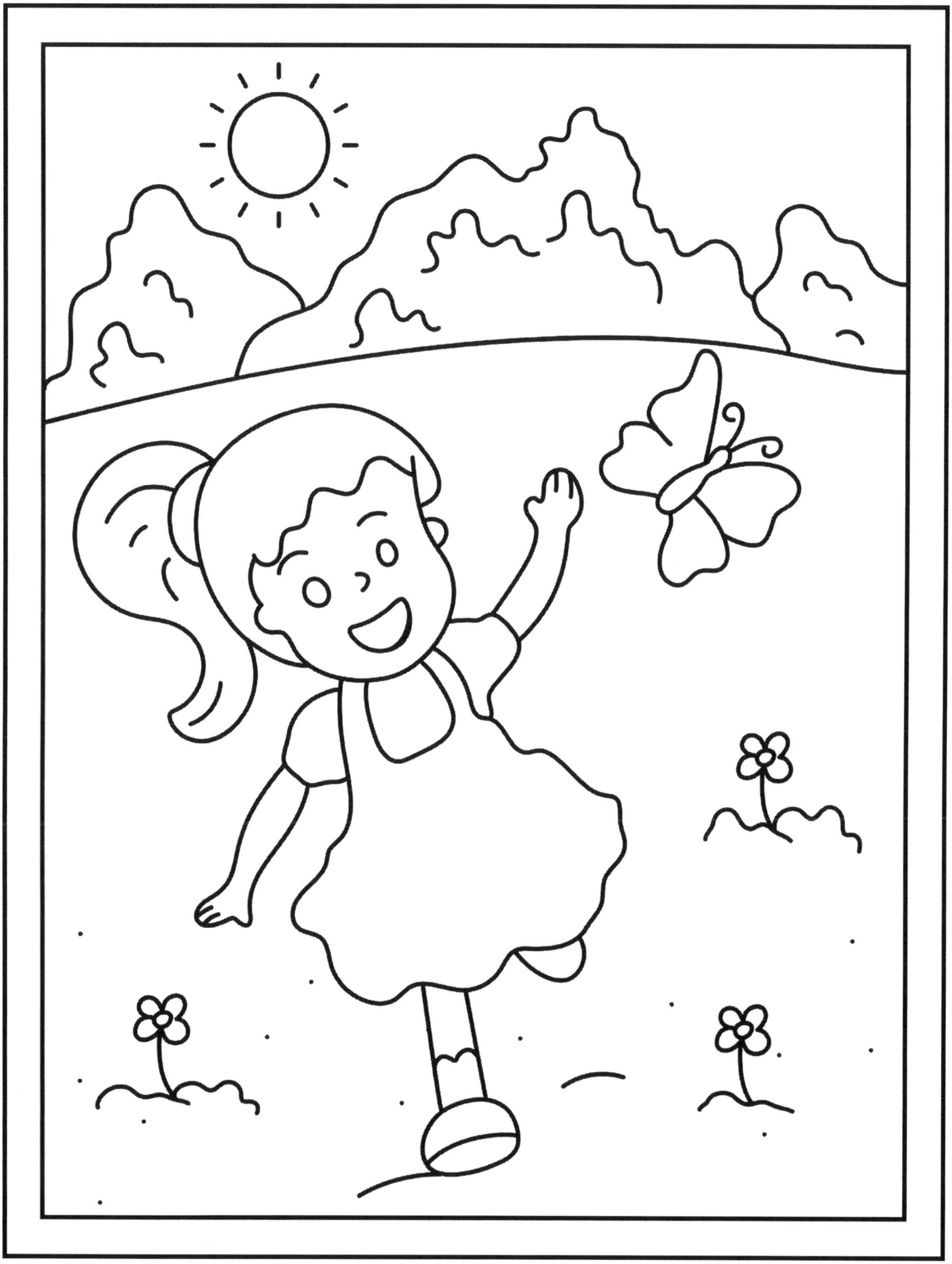

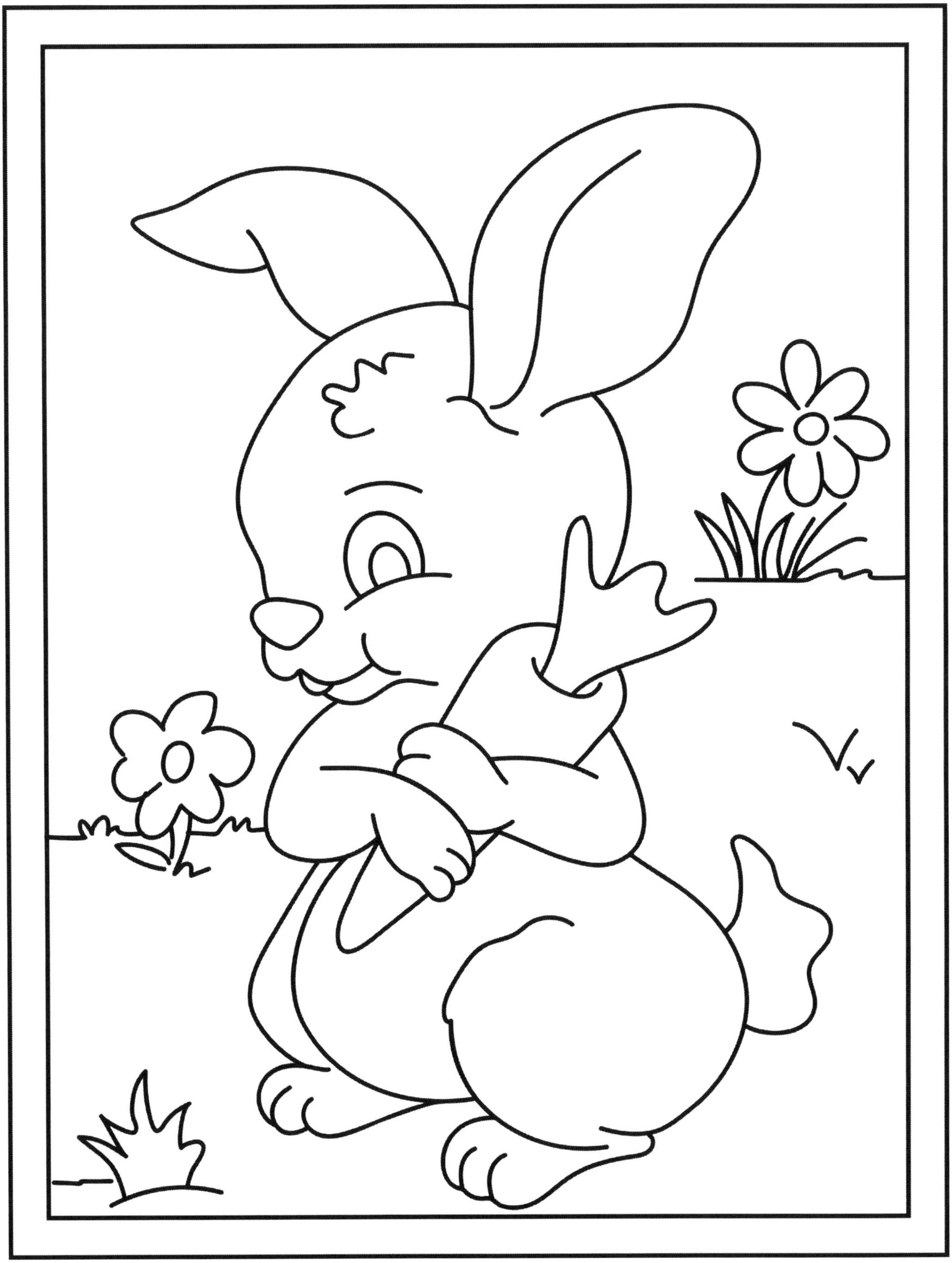

Made in the USA
Las Vegas, NV
26 February 2022

44614363R00015